What Animals Eat

OMNIVORES

James Benefield

Heinemann
LIBRARY

Chicago, Illinois

To contact Capstone Global Library, please call 800-747-4992, or visit our web site
www.capstonepub.com

Edited by James Benefield and Amanda Robbins
Designed by Richard Parker
Picture research by Svetlana Zhurkin
Production by Helen McCreath
Originated by Capstone Global Library Ltd
Printed and bound in China by Leo Paper Group

18 17 16 15 14
10 9 8 7 6 5 4 3 2 1

Library of Congress Cataloging-in-Publication Data
Benefield, James, author.
  Omnivores / James Benefield.
     pages cm.—(What animals eat)
  ISBN 978-1-4846-0849-4 (hb)—ISBN 978-1-4846-0853-1 (pb)—ISBN 978-1-4846-0861-6 (ebook) 1.
Omnivores—Juvenile literature. 2. Animals—Food—Juvenile literature. I. Title.

  QL756.5.B444 2015
  591.5—dc23   2014013684

This book has been officially leveled by using the F&P Text Level Gradient™ Leveling System.

Acknowledgments
We would like to thank the following for permission to reproduce photographs: Dreamstime: Heiti
Paves, 23 (sap); Minden Pictures: Konrad Wothe, 22; Newscom: Visual&Written/Kike Calvo, 11,
ZUMA Press/Anthony Bannister, 19; Shutterstock: Aleksey Poprugin, 9, 23 (claws), arek_malang, 4,
Bogdan Ionescu, 23 (algae), CreativeNature.nl, 23 (mealworms), Danny Wang, 15, Dmitry Maslov, 17,
Eduard Kyslynskyy, back cover, 8, 13, Galyna Andrushko, cover, hin255, 18, Igor Petrovich Potapov,
7, Ivonne Wierink, 20, Monkey Business Images, 16, Pavel K (footprints), throughout, philippou, 5,
Ralph Loesche, 23 (forest), Svet-lana, 10, Vasily Vishnevskiy, 14, Vlue, 23 (root), warmer, 21, Wild At
Art, 6; SuperStock: Biosphoto, 12.

Every effort has been made to contact copyright holders of material reproduced in this book. Any
omissions will be rectified in subsequent printings if notice is given to the publisher.

Disclaimer
All the Internet addresses (URLs) given in this book were valid at the time of going to press.
However, due to the dynamic nature of the Internet, some addresses may have changed, or sites
may have changed or ceased to exist since publication. While the author and publisher regret any
inconvenience this may cause readers, no responsibility for any such changes can be accepted by
either the author or the publisher.

Contents

Some words are shown in bold, **like this**.
You can find them in the glossary on page 23.

What Do Animals Eat?

You need to eat the right food to live and grow. Animals need the right food, too. Different animals eat different things.

Omnivores eat both plants and meat.
Carnivores only eat meat. Herbivores only
eat plants.

What Is an Omnivore?

Omnivores are animals that eat many kinds of meat, such as insects, birds, and fish. Brown bears live near rivers to catch fish to eat. They also eat berries.

Omnivores eat food from plants, such as fruits, vegetables, or grains. Chipmunks eat insects, but they also eat food such as seeds.

How Do Omnivores Get Food?

Omnivores eat different things, so they have different ways to get food. A pig has a strong sense of smell, which helps it to find food.

Look at the **claws** on this hedgehog. These claws help it dig through soil to find food, such as insects or **roots**.

How Do Omnivores Eat Food?

Omnivores need different types of teeth. This raccoon has some sharp teeth to tear meat. The sharp teeth also help it to catch its food.

But omnivores need the right teeth to eat plants, too. These are flat teeth. They help omnivores to grind their food.

Are Omnivores Predators or Prey?

Omnivores that hunt animals are called predators. Omnivores that are hunted are called prey. Which animal is the predator in this picture?

An omnivore can be both predator and prey.
For example, a mouse eats plants and insects.
But a cat might eat this mouse.

Omnivores All Around

Omnivores are everywhere, including in the air. Many birds are omnivores. A woodpecker eats insects and also drinks **sap** from trees.

There are omnivores in the sea, too. Crabs are omnivores that spend time in the sea. Crabs eat **algae**, but they also eat worms.

Can You Find an Omnivore in Your Home?

The omnivore you know best is you! A lot of people eat both meat and vegetables.

Rats are omnivores that some people keep as pets. They eat fruits and vegetables, but also meaty treats such as **mealworms**.

Omnivores in Danger

The cassowary's home in Australia is in danger. It lives in **forests**, but humans are cutting some of the trees down. This makes it hard to find food.

The armadillo lizard has a special way to stop being eaten. It can roll up into a ball. Its shell makes it hard for predators to eat it.

Dangerous Omnivores

Some omnivores are dangerous. Flies eat lots of things, from old fruit to poo! This can spread germs to other animals.

This slow loris is an omnivore that makes poison. It makes the poison in its arms. It licks the poison before biting its predators.

Omnivores Are All Different

Some omnivores are predators, some are prey, and some are both. They all look different, but this opossum has things that many omnivores have.

Eyes that can see predators all around, but also prey in front

sharp teeth

grinding teeth

claws

Picture Glossary

algae
plant-like seaweeds. Crabs eat algae.

claw
hard, pointy, and curvy end to an animal's finger or toe

forest
large place with lots of trees, and bigger than a wood

mealworm
tiny, newborn, worm-like animal that grows up into a meal beetle

root
underground part of a plant that uses water and nutrients from the soil

sap
sticky, sugary water that comes out of trees and plants

Find Out More

Books

Kalman, Bobbie. *Rapping About What Animals Eat* (Rapping About). New York: Crabtree, 2012.

Stones, Brenda. *What Animals Eat* (Kingfisher Readers). New York: Kingfisher, 2012.

Internet sites

Facthound offers a safe, fun way to find Internet sites related to this book. All of the sites on Facthound have been researched by our staff.

Here's all you do:

Visit www.facthound.com

Type in this code: 9781484608494

Index